50 Juice, Broth and Beyond Recipes

By: Kelly Johnson

Table of Contents

- Golden Ginger Elixir
- Spicy Bone Broth Boost
- Green Zen Cleanse
- Beetroot Revival Juice
- Citrus Immunity Shot
- Miso Mushroom Broth
- Turmeric Glow Tonic
- Charcoal Lemon Detox
- Matcha Mint Cooler
- Carrot Curry Broth
- Blueberry Basil Spritz
- Spicy Tomato Sipper
- Coconut Lemongrass Broth
- Aloe Cucumber Splash
- Chaga Mushroom Brew
- Fennel Apple Cleanse
- Smoky Paprika Veg Broth

- Hibiscus Hydration Tonic
- Garlic Ginger Soup Shot
- Celery Cilantro Flush
- Spiced Apple Bone Broth
- Pineapple Cayenne Cleanser
- Watermelon Rose Refresher
- Saffron Ginger Broth
- Avocado Cucumber Smooth Sip
- Cinnamon Carrot Tonic
- Thai Basil Broth Bowl
- Blackberry Sage Elixir
- Turmeric Tamarind Tonic
- Minted Melon Splash
- Shiitake Kombu Broth
- Strawberry Jalapeño Juice
- Reishi Root Power Brew
- Lemongrass Chili Broth
- Apple Cider Sage Sipper
- Cilantro Lime Veg Broth

- Grapefruit Ginger Fizz
- Sun-Dried Tomato Broth
- Orange Fennel Flush
- Lavender Lemon Water
- Smoky Beet Borscht Shot
- Kiwi Spinach Squeeze
- Sweet Corn Ginger Broth
- Guava Mint Cooler
- Anise-Spiced Bone Broth
- Tangerine Thyme Elixir
- Kombucha Veggie Fusion
- Pomegranate Citrus Splash
- Sweet Potato Cinnamon Broth
- Spirulina Hydration Shot

Golden Ginger Elixir

Ingredients

- 1 inch fresh ginger root (grated)
- 1 cup coconut water
- 1 tsp turmeric powder
- 1 tsp honey or agave
- Juice of 1/2 lemon
- Pinch of black pepper

Instructions

1. In a small saucepan, warm the coconut water.
2. Stir in ginger, turmeric, honey, and lemon juice.
3. Simmer for 5–10 mins, then strain.
4. Add a pinch of black pepper, stir, and sip!

Spicy Bone Broth Boost

Ingredients

- 2 cups bone broth (beef or chicken)
- 1/2 tsp cayenne pepper
- 1 tbsp apple cider vinegar
- 1 clove garlic, minced
- Fresh cilantro for garnish

Instructions

1. Heat the bone broth in a pot.
2. Stir in cayenne, vinegar, and garlic, let simmer for 5–7 minutes.
3. Pour into a cup, garnish with cilantro, and enjoy the heat!

Green Zen Cleanse

Ingredients

- 1 cucumber, peeled
- 1 cup spinach or kale
- 1 green apple, cored
- Juice of 1/2 lemon
- 1/2 tsp spirulina powder (optional)
- 1 cup water or coconut water

Instructions

1. Blend cucumber, spinach, apple, lemon, and spirulina (if using) with water.
2. Strain or serve as is, chilled.

Beetroot Revival Juice

Ingredients

- 1 medium beetroot, peeled
- 1 carrot
- 1 apple
- 1/2 lemon, juiced
- 1-inch ginger root, peeled
- 1/2 cup water

Instructions

1. Juice the beetroot, carrot, apple, and ginger.
2. Add lemon juice and water, stir well, and serve chilled.

Citrus Immunity Shot

Ingredients

- Juice of 1 orange
- Juice of 1/2 lemon
- 1 tbsp raw honey
- 1/2 inch fresh ginger root, grated
- Pinch of cayenne pepper

Instructions

1. Combine citrus juices, honey, ginger, and cayenne in a shot glass.
2. Stir well and take it like a boost for your immune system!

Miso Mushroom Broth

Ingredients

- 2 cups vegetable broth
- 1/2 cup miso paste (white or red)
- 1 cup sliced mushrooms (shiitake or cremini)
- 1 tsp soy sauce
- Fresh scallions for garnish

Instructions

1. Heat vegetable broth in a pot.
2. Stir in miso paste, soy sauce, and mushrooms, simmer for 10 minutes.
3. Garnish with scallions and serve warm.

Turmeric Glow Tonic
Ingredients

- 1 cup warm water
- 1 tsp turmeric powder
- 1/2 tsp cinnamon
- 1 tsp honey
- Juice of 1/2 lemon
- Pinch of black pepper

Instructions

1. Stir turmeric, cinnamon, honey, and lemon juice into warm water.
2. Add black pepper, stir well, and drink it while it's cozy and warming.

Charcoal Lemon Detox

Ingredients

- 1/2 tsp activated charcoal powder
- Juice of 1 lemon
- 1 tsp maple syrup
- 1 cup water

Instructions

1. Stir activated charcoal into water.
2. Add lemon juice and maple syrup, mix well, and sip slowly for detox goodness!

Matcha Mint Cooler

Ingredients

- 1 tsp matcha powder
- 1/2 cup hot water
- 1/2 cup coconut milk or almond milk
- 1 tbsp honey or sweetener of choice
- Fresh mint leaves for garnish

Instructions

1. Dissolve matcha in hot water, then stir in honey.
2. Pour coconut milk over ice, then add matcha mix.
3. Garnish with mint and serve.

Carrot Curry Broth

Ingredients

- 2 carrots, peeled and chopped
- 2 cups vegetable broth
- 1 tsp curry powder
- 1/2 cup coconut milk
- 1 tbsp ginger, grated

Instructions

1. Simmer carrots, vegetable broth, curry powder, and ginger for 15 minutes.
2. Blend until smooth, stir in coconut milk, and serve warm.

Blueberry Basil Spritz
Ingredients

- 1/2 cup fresh blueberries
- 4-5 fresh basil leaves
- 1 tbsp honey or agave
- 1 tbsp lemon juice
- 1 cup sparkling water
- Ice cubes

Instructions

1. Muddle blueberries and basil with honey and lemon juice.
2. Fill a glass with ice, pour the muddled mix over, and top with sparkling water.
3. Stir gently and garnish with extra basil or blueberries.

Spicy Tomato Sipper

Ingredients

- 1 cup tomato juice
- 1/2 tsp hot sauce (adjust to taste)
- 1/4 tsp smoked paprika
- Juice of 1/2 lime
- Celery stalk for garnish

Instructions

1. Mix tomato juice, hot sauce, smoked paprika, and lime juice.
2. Stir well and serve over ice.
3. Garnish with a celery stalk for an extra burst of flavor.

Coconut Lemongrass Broth

Ingredients

- 2 cups coconut water
- 1 stalk lemongrass, chopped
- 1-inch piece fresh ginger, sliced
- 1 tbsp soy sauce or tamari
- 1 tsp honey

Instructions

1. Simmer coconut water, lemongrass, and ginger for 10 minutes.
2. Stir in soy sauce and honey, and strain the broth.
3. Serve warm for a soothing, fragrant experience.

Aloe Cucumber Splash

Ingredients

- 1/2 cucumber, peeled and chopped
- 1/2 cup aloe vera juice
- 1 tbsp lime juice
- 1 tsp honey or agave
- 1 cup cold water

Instructions

1. Blend cucumber, aloe vera juice, lime juice, and honey.
2. Add water to adjust the consistency, blend again, and serve over ice.

Chaga Mushroom Brew

Ingredients

- 1 tsp chaga mushroom powder
- 1 cup hot water
- 1 tbsp honey or maple syrup
- 1/4 tsp cinnamon (optional)

Instructions

1. Mix chaga mushroom powder with hot water, stirring to dissolve.
2. Add honey and cinnamon (if using), stir, and enjoy as a warm, earthy brew.

Fennel Apple Cleanse

Ingredients

- 1/2 fennel bulb, chopped
- 1 apple, cored and chopped
- 1/2 lemon, juiced
- 1/2 tsp ginger, grated
- 1 cup cold water

Instructions

1. Blend fennel, apple, lemon juice, and ginger with water.
2. Strain if desired, and serve chilled.

Smoky Paprika Veg Broth

Ingredients

- 2 cups vegetable broth
- 1/4 tsp smoked paprika
- 1/2 tsp garlic powder
- 1/4 tsp cayenne pepper
- Fresh parsley for garnish

Instructions

1. Heat the vegetable broth in a pot.
2. Stir in smoked paprika, garlic powder, and cayenne pepper.
3. Simmer for 5–10 minutes, garnish with parsley, and serve warm.

Hibiscus Hydration Tonic

Ingredients

- 2 tbsp dried hibiscus flowers
- 1 cup boiling water
- 1 tbsp honey or agave
- Juice of 1/2 lime
- Ice cubes

Instructions

1. Steep hibiscus flowers in boiling water for 5 minutes.
2. Strain and stir in honey and lime juice.
3. Serve chilled over ice for a refreshing tonic.

Garlic Ginger Soup Shot

Ingredients

- 1 clove garlic, minced
- 1 tsp fresh ginger, grated
- 1 cup vegetable broth
- 1 tbsp lemon juice
- Pinch of cayenne pepper

Instructions

1. Sauté garlic and ginger for 1–2 minutes until fragrant.
2. Add vegetable broth, bring to a simmer, and cook for 5 minutes.
3. Stir in lemon juice and cayenne, strain, and serve as a shot!

Celery Cilantro Flush

Ingredients

- 2 stalks celery, chopped
- 1/2 cup fresh cilantro
- 1/2 lime, juiced
- 1/2 cucumber, peeled
- 1 cup cold water

Instructions

1. Blend celery, cilantro, lime juice, cucumber, and water.
2. Strain if desired, and serve over ice for a refreshing cleanse.

Spiced Apple Bone Broth

Ingredients

- 2 cups bone broth (chicken or beef)
- 1 medium apple, chopped
- 1 cinnamon stick
- 2 cloves
- 1 tsp honey or maple syrup
- Pinch of ground nutmeg

Instructions

1. Heat bone broth in a pot with apple, cinnamon stick, cloves, and nutmeg.
2. Simmer for 10 minutes.
3. Remove spices, stir in honey, and serve warm for a cozy, nourishing drink.

Pineapple Cayenne Cleanser
Ingredients

- 1 cup fresh pineapple chunks
- 1/2 tsp cayenne pepper
- 1 tbsp lemon juice
- 1 cup water
- Ice cubes

Instructions

1. Blend pineapple, cayenne, lemon juice, and water until smooth.
2. Pour over ice and serve for a sweet and spicy cleanse.

Watermelon Rose Refresher

Ingredients

- 2 cups watermelon, chopped
- 1 tbsp rose water
- 1 tbsp lime juice
- 1 tsp honey or agave
- Ice cubes

Instructions

1. Blend watermelon, rose water, lime juice, and honey until smooth.
2. Serve over ice and garnish with extra watermelon or mint leaves.

Saffron Ginger Broth

Ingredients

- 2 cups vegetable broth
- 1 pinch saffron threads
- 1 tsp fresh ginger, grated
- 1 tbsp lemon juice
- Fresh cilantro for garnish

Instructions

1. Heat vegetable broth, saffron, and ginger in a pot.
2. Simmer for 5–7 minutes.
3. Stir in lemon juice and garnish with cilantro before serving.

Avocado Cucumber Smooth Sip

Ingredients

- 1/2 ripe avocado
- 1/2 cucumber, peeled
- 1 tbsp lime juice
- 1 cup coconut water
- 1 tsp honey or agave
- Ice cubes

Instructions

1. Blend avocado, cucumber, lime juice, coconut water, and honey until smooth.
2. Serve chilled over ice for a creamy, hydrating treat.

Cinnamon Carrot Tonic

Ingredients

- 2 large carrots, chopped
- 1 cinnamon stick
- 1 tbsp honey
- 1 cup water
- 1/2 tsp ground ginger

Instructions

1. Simmer carrots, cinnamon stick, and ginger in water for 10 minutes.
2. Remove cinnamon stick and blend until smooth.
3. Stir in honey and serve warm or chilled.

Thai Basil Broth Bowl

Ingredients

- 2 cups vegetable broth
- 1 tbsp Thai basil, chopped
- 1 tbsp soy sauce or tamari
- 1 tsp fresh ginger, grated
- 1/2 lime, juiced

Instructions

1. Heat vegetable broth, soy sauce, ginger, and lime juice in a pot.
2. Simmer for 5–7 minutes, then stir in Thai basil.
3. Serve warm as a fragrant, flavorful broth bowl.

Blackberry Sage Elixir

Ingredients

- 1 cup fresh blackberries
- 1/4 cup fresh sage leaves
- 1 tbsp honey or maple syrup
- 1 tbsp lemon juice
- 1 cup water

Instructions

1. Blend blackberries, sage, honey, lemon juice, and water until smooth.
2. Strain and serve chilled over ice for a refreshing, herbal sip.

Turmeric Tamarind Tonic

Ingredients

- 1/2 tsp turmeric powder
- 1 tbsp tamarind paste
- 1 tbsp honey or agave
- 1 cup warm water
- Pinch of black pepper

Instructions

1. Stir turmeric, tamarind paste, honey, and black pepper into warm water.
2. Mix well and sip slowly for an anti-inflammatory boost.

Minted Melon Splash

Ingredients

- 2 cups melon (cantaloupe or honeydew), chopped
- 1/4 cup fresh mint leaves
- 1 tbsp lime juice
- 1 tsp honey or agave
- Ice cubes

Instructions

1. Blend melon, mint, lime juice, and honey until smooth.
2. Serve over ice and garnish with mint leaves for a refreshing splash.

Shiitake Kombu Broth

Ingredients

- 2 cups vegetable broth
- 1/2 cup dried shiitake mushrooms
- 1 sheet kombu seaweed
- 1 tbsp soy sauce or tamari
- 1 tsp sesame oil

Instructions

1. Simmer vegetable broth, shiitake mushrooms, and kombu for 10–15 minutes.
2. Remove kombu, stir in soy sauce and sesame oil, and serve warm.

Strawberry Jalapeño Juice

Ingredients

- 1 cup fresh strawberries
- 1/2 jalapeño, deseeded
- 1 tbsp lime juice
- 1 tsp honey or agave
- 1 cup cold water

Instructions

1. Blend strawberries, jalapeño, lime juice, honey, and water until smooth.
2. Strain if desired and serve over ice for a sweet and spicy kick.

Reishi Root Power Brew

Ingredients

- 1 tsp reishi mushroom powder
- 1 cup hot water
- 1 tsp honey or maple syrup
- 1/2 tsp ground cinnamon
- 1/4 tsp ground nutmeg

Instructions

1. Stir reishi mushroom powder, honey, cinnamon, and nutmeg into hot water.
2. Mix well and enjoy as a calming, immunity-boosting brew.

Lemongrass Chili Broth

Ingredients

- 2 cups vegetable broth
- 1 stalk lemongrass, chopped
- 1 small chili pepper, chopped
- 1 tsp soy sauce
- 1 tsp lime juice

Instructions

1. Simmer vegetable broth with lemongrass and chili pepper for 10 minutes.
2. Stir in soy sauce and lime juice, then strain and serve warm for a zesty, spicy broth.

Apple Cider Sage Sipper

Ingredients

- 1 cup apple cider vinegar
- 1 cup water
- 1 tbsp fresh sage leaves
- 1 tbsp honey or agave
- 1/2 tsp ground cinnamon

Instructions

1. Heat water and apple cider vinegar in a pot with sage and cinnamon.
2. Simmer for 5 minutes, then strain and stir in honey.
3. Serve warm for a detoxifying, soothing sipper.

Cilantro Lime Veg Broth

Ingredients

- 2 cups vegetable broth
- 1/4 cup fresh cilantro, chopped
- Juice of 1 lime
- 1 garlic clove, minced
- Pinch of sea salt

Instructions

1. Heat vegetable broth with garlic and sea salt.
2. Stir in cilantro and lime juice, simmer for 5 minutes.
3. Strain and serve warm as a fresh, herbaceous broth.

Grapefruit Ginger Fizz

Ingredients

- 1/2 cup fresh grapefruit juice
- 1 tsp fresh ginger, grated
- 1 tbsp honey or agave
- 1 cup sparkling water
- Ice cubes

Instructions

1. Mix grapefruit juice, ginger, and honey in a shaker.
2. Pour over ice and top with sparkling water.
3. Stir gently and enjoy the refreshing fizz.

Sun-Dried Tomato Broth
Ingredients

- 2 cups vegetable broth
- 1/4 cup sun-dried tomatoes, chopped
- 1 tbsp olive oil
- 1 tbsp balsamic vinegar
- Fresh basil for garnish

Instructions

1. Simmer vegetable broth with sun-dried tomatoes for 10 minutes.
2. Stir in olive oil and balsamic vinegar.
3. Strain and serve warm, garnished with fresh basil.

Orange Fennel Flush

Ingredients

- 1 orange, peeled
- 1/2 fennel bulb, chopped
- 1 tbsp honey or agave
- 1 cup cold water

Instructions

1. Blend orange, fennel, and honey with cold water until smooth.
2. Strain if desired, and serve chilled as a refreshing flush.

Lavender Lemon Water

Ingredients

- 1 tbsp dried lavender flowers
- 1 lemon, sliced
- 1 cup hot water
- 1 tsp honey or agave

Instructions

1. Steep lavender flowers in hot water for 5 minutes.
2. Stir in honey and add lemon slices.
3. Serve warm for a calming and fragrant drink.

Smoky Beet Borscht Shot

Ingredients

- 1 small beetroot, peeled and chopped
- 1/2 tsp smoked paprika
- 1 tbsp lemon juice
- 1/2 cup vegetable broth
- 1 tsp sour cream (optional)

Instructions

1. Simmer beetroot with smoked paprika in vegetable broth for 10 minutes.
2. Blend until smooth, strain, and stir in lemon juice.
3. Serve in shot glasses, garnished with sour cream if desired.

Kiwi Spinach Squeeze
Ingredients

- 2 ripe kiwis, peeled
- 1/2 cup spinach leaves
- 1 tbsp lime juice
- 1 tsp honey or agave
- 1 cup cold water

Instructions

1. Blend kiwis, spinach, lime juice, honey, and cold water until smooth.
2. Strain if desired, and serve chilled for a refreshing, nutrient-packed squeeze.

Sweet Corn Ginger Broth

Ingredients

- 2 cups vegetable broth
- 1 cup sweet corn kernels
- 1-inch piece fresh ginger, grated
- 1 tbsp soy sauce
- 1 tsp lime juice

Instructions

1. Simmer vegetable broth with corn and ginger for 10 minutes.
2. Stir in soy sauce and lime juice.
3. Strain and serve warm for a sweet, spicy, and comforting broth.

Guava Mint Cooler

Ingredients

- 1 cup fresh guava, peeled and chopped
- 1/4 cup fresh mint leaves
- 1 tbsp lime juice
- 1 tsp honey or agave
- 1 cup sparkling water
- Ice cubes

Instructions

1. Blend guava, mint, lime juice, and honey until smooth.
2. Pour over ice and top with sparkling water for a refreshing, tropical cooler.

Anise-Spiced Bone Broth

Ingredients

- 2 cups bone broth (chicken or beef)
- 1 star anise
- 1 cinnamon stick
- 1 tbsp soy sauce
- 1/2 tsp ground ginger

Instructions

1. Simmer bone broth with star anise, cinnamon stick, and ground ginger for 10 minutes.
2. Stir in soy sauce, strain, and serve warm for a deeply flavored, aromatic broth.

Tangerine Thyme Elixir
Ingredients

- 2 tangerines, peeled and juiced
- 1 tbsp fresh thyme leaves
- 1 tsp honey or agave
- 1 cup water
- Ice cubes

Instructions

1. Mix tangerine juice, thyme, honey, and water together.
2. Pour over ice and serve as a sweet and herbal elixir.

Kombucha Veggie Fusion

Ingredients

- 1 cup kombucha (your favorite flavor)
- 1/2 cup carrot juice
- 1/4 cup cucumber juice
- 1 tbsp lemon juice
- Ice cubes

Instructions

1. Mix kombucha with carrot juice, cucumber juice, and lemon juice.
2. Serve over ice for a fizzy, veggie-packed refreshment.

Pomegranate Citrus Splash

Ingredients

- 1/2 cup pomegranate juice
- 1/2 cup orange juice
- 1 tbsp lemon juice
- 1 tsp honey or agave
- Ice cubes

Instructions

1. Mix pomegranate juice, orange juice, lemon juice, and honey.
2. Serve over ice for a tangy, antioxidant-rich drink.

Sweet Potato Cinnamon Broth

Ingredients

- 2 cups vegetable broth
- 1 small sweet potato, peeled and cubed
- 1 cinnamon stick
- 1 tbsp maple syrup
- Pinch of salt

Instructions

1. Simmer vegetable broth with sweet potato and cinnamon stick for 10–15 minutes.
2. Blend until smooth, then stir in maple syrup and a pinch of salt.
3. Serve warm for a comforting, mildly sweet broth.

Spirulina Hydration Shot

Ingredients

- 1/2 tsp spirulina powder
- 1/4 cup coconut water
- 1 tbsp lime juice
- 1 tsp honey or agave

Instructions

1. Stir spirulina powder into coconut water until dissolved.
2. Add lime juice and honey, mix well, and serve as a nutrient-dense shot.

www.ingramcontent.com/pod-product-compliance
Lightning Source LLC
LaVergne TN
LVHW081326060526
838201LV00055B/2484